CREATING ART IN NATURE

BY ABBY COLICH

BLUE OWL
BOOKS

TIPS FOR CAREGIVERS

Social and emotional learning (SEL) helps children manage emotions, learn how to feel empathy, create and achieve goals, and make good decisions. One goal of teaching SEL skills is to help children care for themselves, others, and the world around them. The more time children spend in nature and the more they learn about it, the more likely they will be to appreciate it and receive its emotional benefits.

BEFORE READING

Talk to the reader about different art forms, such as drawing, crafting, writing, and performing. Then discuss how nature can inspire different art forms.

Discuss: What do you like to create? Have you ever created art outside or with items from nature?

AFTER READING

Talk to the reader about the benefits of creating art and spending time in nature.

Discuss: How does creating art make you feel? How does spending time in nature make you feel? What are the benefits of creating art in nature?

SEL GOAL

Children may struggle with processing their emotions, and they may lack accessible tools to help them do so. Explain to children that creating art can help them work through emotions, express themselves, and feel pride. Creating art in nature can enhance these benefits by helping them be more mindful. Help children come up with ways they can incorporate nature into their artwork by using nature as inspiration, creating art outside, or using items from nature to create art.

TABLE OF CONTENTS

CHAPTER 1
Art and Nature 4

CHAPTER 2
Feel Inspired 10

CHAPTER 3
Go Create! 14

GOALS AND TOOLS
Grow with Goals 22
Mindfulness Exercise 22
Glossary 23
To Learn More 23
Index 24

CHAPTER 1

ART AND NATURE

How do you practice **creativity**? Do you write stories or poetry? Do you sculpt or build things? Some people like to paint or draw. Dancing and acting are also forms of art.

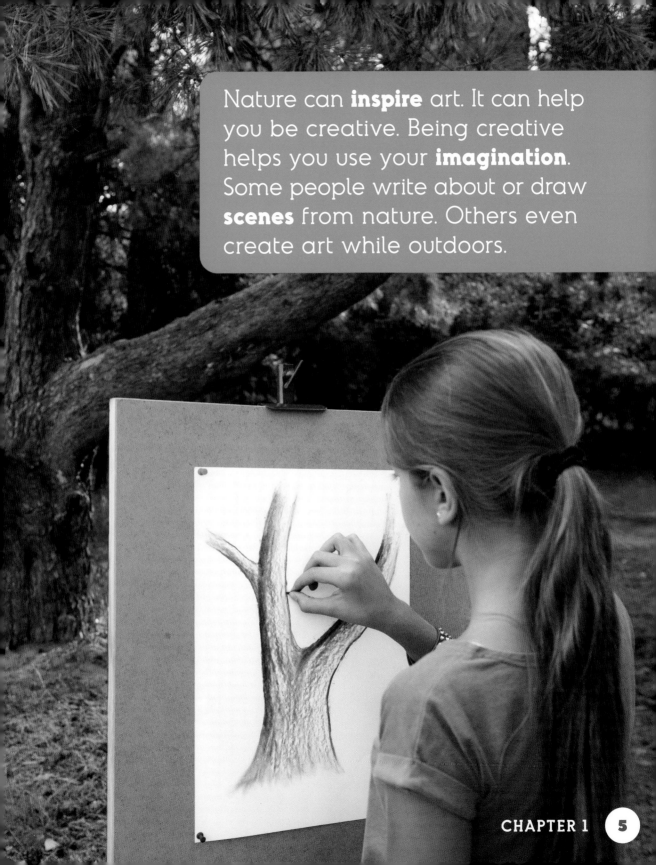

Nature can **inspire** art. It can help you be creative. Being creative helps you use your **imagination**. Some people write about or draw **scenes** from nature. Others even create art while outdoors.

Spending time in nature is good for you. It can help you practice **mindfulness**. It can help you **focus** and feel less **stressed**. This helps you **express** yourself.

Creating art in or about nature can be easy. First, decide what you want to create. Then, gather the right supplies. Make sure you have enough space and time. If you feel rushed, you may get **frustrated** and feel less creative.

PHOTOGRAPH NATURE

Try taking pictures of nature. You can look at them later when you want to feel inspired but can't go outside.

CHAPTER 2

FEEL INSPIRED

Nature can inspire us in many ways. It can also help limit **distractions**. Put away your **devices**. Pay attention to what you see, hear, and smell. See what new ideas come to mind!

Take a walk in nature and focus only on your movements. Or find a spot to sit. Focus on your breathing. Keep your body still. Try to slow your thoughts. This will help you feel closer to nature and more inspired.

This branch looks like a centipede. Could I make bug crafts out of other plants?

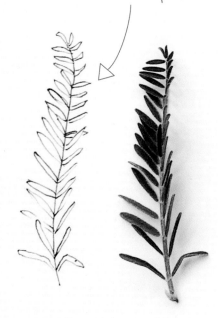

Purple flowers are my favorite!
They make me happy!

Keeping a nature journal is one way to be creative. Write down your ideas. You can collect items you find outside and attach them to the pages. You can also write about or draw pictures of what you see outside.

ITEMS FROM NATURE

If you want to collect items from nature for a craft, don't take more than you need. Never take flowers or leaves from living plants. Look for them on the ground after they have fallen off.

CHAPTER 3

GO CREATE!

Figure out what from nature inspires you. Focus on what is around you. What do you notice? Is it the colors of a flower? Maybe you hear the sounds of a bird. Maybe you notice how bright and warm the sun is. Paying attention to details can help you feel inspired.

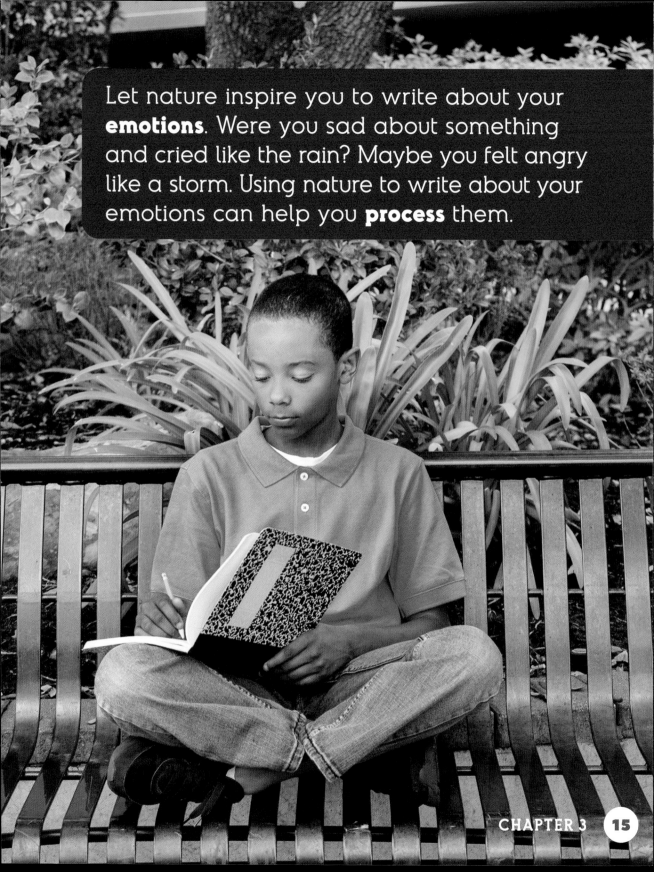

Let nature inspire you to write about your **emotions**. Were you sad about something and cried like the rain? Maybe you felt angry like a storm. Using nature to write about your emotions can help you **process** them.

Crafting and creating in nature can help you work through your emotions. If you are looking for strength, build a tree or mountain out of clay. If you are stressed, use chalk to make fast, dark lines on the pavement until you feel better. If you are happy, find bright objects outside to inspire your own colorful painting.

WATCH THE CLOUDS

Take a moment to watch a cloud in the sky. Do you notice its slight movements? Like the clouds, your emotions will change. They won't last forever.

Paying attention to your senses in nature can help you be creative. Write about something that is smooth like a rock or rough like bark. Listen to a bird chirping and use it to inspire you to write a song. Or create a dance or **yoga** routine that includes movements or poses inspired by the **wildlife** around you.

If you want, share your art with others. Let them know what in nature inspired you. Sharing your art may help you grow closer to others. You could even work on an art project together!

KEEP TRYING!

Sometimes you may feel stuck. That is OK. Take some deep breaths. Try to imagine what you want to create. Or create something else. Keep practicing and trying new things.

GOALS AND TOOLS

GROW WITH GOALS

Spending time and creating art in nature can help you be more creative and mindful.

Goal: Think of a word that describes how you feel right now. Then think of something in nature that reminds you of this word. Draw, sculpt, or create it.

Goal: Schedule time at least once a week to create something. Just doodling or coloring for a few minutes can help you feel less stressed and more focused.

Goal: Go on a nature walk. See how many different patterns, shapes, and colors you can spot. Then choose a few to re-create in your artwork.

MINDFULNESS EXERCISE

What is your favorite place in nature? It could be the spot where you sit under a tree, a pond where you watch ducks, or a path where you walk or bike. Create something that reminds you of that spot, such as a painting or a sculpture, or write a few words about it. Place what you created in your bedroom or somewhere you will see it often. When you feel upset, look at what you created. Picture yourself in your favorite spot. It might help you feel better.

GLOSSARY

creativity
The ability to make new things or think of new ideas.

devices
Pieces of equipment with computers inside, such as smartphones or tablets.

distractions
Things that draw a person's attention away from something.

emotions
Feelings, such as happiness, sadness, or anger.

express
To show what you feel or think with words, writing, or actions.

focus
To concentrate on something.

frustrated
Annoyed or angry.

imagination
The ability to think of new things.

inspire
To influence and encourage someone to achieve or do something.

mindfulness
A mentality achieved by focusing on the present moment and calmly recognizing and accepting your feelings, thoughts, and sensations.

process
To gain an understanding or acceptance of something.

scenes
Views or sights that look like pictures.

stressed
Experiencing mental or emotional strain.

wildlife
Living things, especially animals, that live in their natural habitats.

yoga
A system of exercises and meditation that helps people control their minds and bodies and become physically fit.

TO LEARN MORE

Finding more information is as easy as 1, 2, 3.

1. Go to www.factsurfer.com

2. Enter "**creatingartinnature**" into the search box.

3. Choose your book to see a list of websites.

INDEX

acting 4

breathing 11, 20

build 4, 16

chalk 16

clay 16

colors 14, 16

creativity 4, 5, 8, 13, 19

dancing 4, 19

devices 10

distractions 10

draw 4, 5, 13

emotions 15, 16

flowers 13, 14

imagination 5, 20

inspire 5, 8, 10, 11, 14, 15, 16, 19, 20

mindfulness 7

movements 11, 16, 19

nature journal 13

paint 4, 16

sculpt 4

thoughts 11

wildlife 19

write 4, 5, 13, 15, 19

yoga 19

Blue Owl Books are published by Jump!, 5357 Penn Avenue South, Minneapolis, MN 55419, www.jumplibrary.com

Copyright © 2021 Jump! International copyright reserved in all countries. No part of this book may be reproduced in any form without written permission from the publisher.

Library of Congress Cataloging-in-Publication Data

Names: Colich, Abby, author.
Title: Creating art in nature / Abby Colich.
Description: Minneapolis, MN: Jump!, Inc., [2021]
Series: Nature heals | Includes index. | Audience: Ages 7–10
Identifiers: LCCN 2020041937 (print)
LCCN 2020041938 (ebook)
ISBN 9781645278344 (hardcover)
ISBN 9781645278351 (paperback)
ISBN 9781645278368 (ebook)
Subjects: LCSH: Arts–Therapeutic use–Juvenile literature. | Healing–Psychological aspects. | Nature.
Classification: LCC RC489.A72 C65 2021 (print) | LCC RC489.A72 (ebook) | DDC 616.89/1656–dc23
LC record available at https://lccn.loc.gov/2020041937
LC ebook record available at https://lccn.loc.gov/2020041938

Editor: Eliza Leahy
Designer: Michelle Sonnek

Photo Credits: Evgeny Karandaev/Shutterstock, cover; Shutterstock, 1, 3; Jan H Andersen/Shutterstock, 4; Nataliia Budianska/Shutterstock, 5; HopeBy/Shutterstock, 6–7; p_ponomareva/Shutterstock, 8–9; AnnGaysorn/Shutterstock, 10; nano/iStock, 11; Tanya_Tatiana/Shutterstock, 12–13; TinnaPong/Shutterstock, 14; fstop123/iStock, 15; shablovskyistock/Shutterstock, 16–17; BlueOrange Studio/Shutterstock, 18–19; Ronnachai Palas/Shutterstock, 20–21.

Printed in the United States of America at Corporate Graphics in North Mankato, Minnesota.